# Spark Your Youth

Display

Only
Contact Author
Anna Willard
for your copy

Book

www. annawillard.com/resources

ANNA WILLARD

# Spark Your Youth

A 21-DAY FITSPIRATIONAL TO GIVE
YOU HOPE AND THE POWER TO
BELIEVE

# IronWillTrain

HOPE

DREAM

BELIEVE

# Dedications

To my family who taught me there is always hope
and the importance of my dreams.

To Kelly McAleer* who introduced me to basketball
and more importantly to living a life full of passion.

To Portia* who always gave me the perfect amount of
excitement to continue my journey
chasing my dreams

*These two beautiful souls are not physically here with us today,
but the way in which they lived their lives provided me this belief
of something greater than life itself.

# Table of Contents

# Preface

It is my honor and privilege to tell you how both Kelly and Portia continue to give me Hope and the power to believe in my dreams.

This book is a 21-day fitspirational to develop the behaviors and motivation you will need to train your mind and soul to focus on your hopes and dreams. It will give you the power to believe in yourself and your inner strength.

As a strength coach, I provide tools for you to successfully reach your physical goals, but you do all the hard work. My job is to guide and direct you toward these goals. The purpose of this 21-day fitspirational is to do the same for your hopes and dreams. During this time, you may find the most challenging weight to lift is the pen. However, keep in mind the satisfaction and reward when achieving something physically challenging, as the reward is much greater if you are willing to do the work for your hopes and dreams.

Each week will focus directly on one of these themes: Hopes, Dreams, and Belief. Some days you will be asked to do a simple writing activity. These activities are designed to help you understand where you may be with your hopes and dreams. Other activities will help you understand how you need to train yourself to achieve them.

Before we start, it is crucial I share with you how I discovered Hope. This is the start of my journey living out my hopes, dreams, and now believing. With this fitspirational, I will be referring to this story and will be sprinkling more anecdotes throughout the 21 days.

# Growing Pains

Ever since I can remember, movement has always captivated me. My mother tells the tory of when I was a toddler and how she would put me in a baby walker. Thinking that I would preoccupy myself in the walker, she would go into the kitchen to make us a meal. To her surprise, I would be crawling into the kitchen while the walker was left in the living room.

Don't ask me how I could have escaped this 1980's baby walker, but I did, and I was always on the move. Being a very active child, my mother enrolled me in ballet thinking this would satisfy my need for movement. Little did she know after a couple months of practice, I was bored with ballet and was attracted to a different sport.

"Mom! Do I have to go?" I pleaded. My cousins Kelly and Johnny echoed this. "Yeah Bitz (my mom), does she have to go? Ballet is too much of a girly thing!" Finally, after many conversations during our drives to ballet practice, I convinced my mom (with the help of my cousins of course) to change my athletics to what I thought was a real sport, basketball.

Kelly and Johnny were more like brothers to me. All my life as I watched them play basketball I told myself that one day I would be just like them! I wanted to play so I could show them that a girl could play the sport too! I started playing in the 3rd grade and was hooked.

Almost five years later, Kelly died at the age of 16 years old at the hands of a driver who was high and drunk. I was 13 years old at the time and was grief-stricken as I watched a slideshow of Kelly's life. As each picture faded into the next, I felt the distance grow and was heartbroken to realize that these pictures, these memories, were all that was left for me. There would be no other chances to create more memories with my cousin Kelly as we grew old together.

Confused with my mixed emotions, all I could focus on was wanting more time with him, but knowing this was impossible. I made a promise to myself that I would play basketball in honor of my cousin. After the funeral, I started journaling and committed to the goal of playing college basketball in honor of him and the impact he had on my life. This gave me a sense of hope.

# A Stormy Struggle

Three years later, I was exactly the same age as Kelly was when he passed away. I unfortunately put myself in a similar situation to the one that ended his life. Many times after my basketball games, my best friend and I would go smoke marijuana, then drive to the movies. We would be so high I would not even remember the drive to the theater or where I was. Other times we would go get drunk and then get high. I didn't realize the dangerous impact these choices could have on my life until one night that changed everything.

My best friend kept pouring me drinks, and I kept drinking them. The last thing I remember her saying was, "finish it!" I chugged the remaining drink, set the cup back on the counter, and then I fell. I had the sensation of continuing to fall . . . and then nothing.

The following morning, I awoke disoriented. Struggling to walk, I had difficulty remembering what happened the night before. *What happened? Why am I so dizzy? How am I going to play in this weekend's basketball tournament? What is going on?*

Disgusted with the smell of my breath and body, I stumbled into the shower. As the water washed away the horrible stench, the memories slowly came back. The memory of "finish it" and the sensation of falling but never hitting the ground jolted me back to the night before. The night replayed itself with the words "finish it" ringing in my mind over and over again. I tried to recall what I had to drink and how much that night, but all I could remember was my friend saying, "finish it," as if she was wishing my life away. After three straight days without an appetite and gingerly learning to walk again, it hit me, I could have died that night from alcohol poisoning.

But I was still alive. I had a chance to change my behavior and refocus on those hopes and dreams that drove me to living my life in a way that would respect my cousin.

# Breakthrough

My first step was to change my perspective. I was so devastated by Kelly's physical absence. I allowed my mind to fixate on his horrible death. This mindset led me down a similar path. A path that obviously had a different ending for me. It was with this realization that I began to fully understand the power of our mind.

I started remembering Kelly's spirit, instead of his death. I remembered how he always made me feel important, how he made me laugh, and how he brought adventure to life. I now allow myself to embrace Kelly's true spirit by living with adventure, always laughing, and embracing my own importance and the importance of others.

This is when Hope came alive in my life.

As your coach, I will be right here alongside you as you start your journey and learn the importance of training your hopes and dreams. This is not an easy task, but you will be stronger in your beliefs as a result of it. I wrote this with you in mind! I will be right here encouraging you and supporting you. As you start Day One, I prayerfully meditate you are able to see how Hope can be alive in your life today!

## ◦◦ DAY 1 ◦◦

# True Hope

True Hope.

By definition, hope is a feeling that something desired may happen. True Hope is when we are able to create a light of service shining with our desires.

You may be asking how can this be so? How can hope be a light of service? We oftentimes become confused with hope's purpose.

Hope is a powerful source of light living in us, wanting to shine through us for each other.

These first two day we'll be diving into what Hope is *not*. I want to make sure you have a clear vision of how Hope can positively affect your life and the lives of others.

For Hope to be alive and active, we need to visit what hope is and, most importantly, what it is not.

Ready?? All right, let's dive in!

- Sit back and remember a time in your life when something amazing happened. Your wedding day, graduation, first job, first kiss, your first . . .

- Think of a time, or an event, where you felt pumped and so excited you couldn't wait for the future!

- Remember how it made you feel, your energy level, your emotions, your excitement, the anticipation.

Now that these feelings are fresh in your memory again, write them down. Take time to describe these experiences and sensations in full detail. Relive these moments to their fullest!

Hold on to these wonderful memories and milestones in your life as we continue.

Sometimes we hope backwards. We long for something from our past to live again in the future; something that once was good (even great) to come back to life. Perhaps it is the very moment you just described to yourself, or something that was exciting and breathtaking and ended up completely the opposite of what you had anticipated.

It could be the hope to right an injustice or sadness in your life. Something as devastating as losing a child due to miscarriage, or the marriage you once had before your divorce, can create attachment injuries that are hard to release. If you were an athlete, did you incur an injury causing you to stop participating in a sport you loved?

These are all moments we know as past - some wonderful and some sad or even tragic. Why do we hope for something we know we cannot change? Why do we spend our time and energy focusing on something that our rational and logical selves know is impossible? How can we hope for something better, something that once was great, but has since turned into a tragedy?

You could be hoping your past mistakes were not mistakes, but instead successes. We find ourselves living in the past, wanting, wishing, and hoping to have done something different.

This is where we start to get confused with the definition of Hope. The purpose of Hope is to be a light living in us and through us. Hope is a guiding force that should lead us forward and not burden us with past losses or fears, for they no longer exist and they cannot be changed.

And hence, this negative energy brought on by the frustration of not being able to "right the wrongs" as it were, turns our spirit and our outlook downward into darkness.

"If only I had done _____ then I would not be dealing with _____." (fill in the blanks)

Have you ever found yourself saying this?

If only I didn't . . . . I would not have miscarried, or I would still be married, or my child would still be talking to me. . . . The list goes on.

I don't know your "if only" moments, but I do know the pain of them. I dealt with my own, "If only I hadn't gotten drunk that one night then I would have been a collegiate athlete." When we play this game of "if only" we go backwards and continue to live in the past, creating a dark obstacle living in the present.

Let me remind you that the essence of true Hope is when we are able to create a light of service shining with our desires. It is living our desires in the present moment. When we understand our desires are a light living in us, through us, and for us, we are able to live the entity of Hope. We are able to shine and embrace the present moment to the fullest.

Let's take a moment and go back to that memory you wrote about. Start to imagine how Hope can play a part in your life today and change your future into something *epic!* Something that is ten times better than the memories you are holding on to, something beyond your own belief.

For today; write/journal about an event that would give you the same, or similar, excitement as your past memory. What is something you always wanted to do? It could be anything from teaching your child to bake a cake to going after the new job you always wanted and getting it! Now allow it to grow beyond your imagination!

You may not be ready for this quite yet. That is ok! I am still on this journey of learning how to embrace something beyond my belief.

This takes time. During these next twenty days you will be given the steps to help you with any barrier that may be blocking your light of Hope from shining.

## ❧ Day 2 ☙

# False Hope

False Hope.

Be honest with yourself. What is it that you hope for in your life from this day forward? Is it marriage? Financial freedom? Children? Graduation? A new job? Freedom from physical pain? A tournament trophy?

Is what you hope for better than the present situation in which you are currently living? If so, that's natural! Let's do another exercise.

At this moment, wherever you may be, what are the top three things that come to mind when you think of your own hopes? Take the next few minutes and write them down below.

1. _____

2. _____

3. _____

Now, have you ever asked yourself why you have these things as your hope(s)? What is the motivation behind the hope? Are they really a reason for Hope or for something else?

Could it be acceptance in a social group? Could it be a sense of completion? Could it give you purpose?

OR . . . Could it be something you idolize in your life?

An idol is a figment of the mind, *a false fantasy.* When we idolize, it comes from a place of self-righteousness.

I ask these questions because I had to be honest with myself about my motivation and for my decisions when defining Hope in my own life and giving Hope a reason. When I asked myself the last question, "Could hope be something you idolize in your life," it felt like a slap in the face! And you may be experiencing the same jolt of awareness. This is good!

These realizations help you question how you define Hope, what you are hoping for, and its motives. The very thing you hope for may be exactly what you need, but what is the motive behind it? Is it to self-serve or to serve others? This is a question only you can answer and it's deep. Take time today and let this sink in a little bit more.

First, let me expand how my goal to honor my cousin soon became an idol in my life.

Why did I want to play college basketball? Why did I think I had to be a collegiate athlete? Why did I think I needed to accomplish these things to give honor to my cousin?

I wanted to be known for my athletics. This goal soon turned into a selfish desire. It soon became about me; my hopes for personal recognition. I lost sight of the purpose and the goal itself. I was so focused on becoming a collegiate athlete that I forgot to become Anna Willard.

I started to seek my worth in my athletic abilities and forgot to use my athletics, my gifts, to honor my cousin. I was so focused on the future outcome that I negated the present moments. It was during those times in practice and in the games I could have honored my cousin.

As a result of misusing my talents, I didn't honor my teammates, my coach, or my family. I used my abilities to seek my own self-importance and worth. I wanted to score the most points, welcome the congratulations for winning the game, and read articles about my amazing performance in the newspaper. I created a false fantasy of becoming a collegiate athlete instead of embracing Anna Willard, and my gifts and talents, in a way that gives back.

I was mentally and physically training my idols and not my hopes.

When defining hope, the teaching methods are similar to strength training. This is the same approach I take when teaching a new lifting skill. I demonstrate the lift with, and without, the proper form. In this instance, I showed you how idols can deceive us from true Hope and, using my story as a mental exercise, demonstrated what not to do when training Hope. Again, I thought I was demonstrating hope when really all throughout my high school years I was seeking and living for an idol.

Much like when we are learning a new exercise, our bodies will want to compensate and do the exercise without proper form. It is through understanding our physical compensation that we are able to perform the exercise correctly. Idols act as compensations when we start training Hope. The first step is becoming aware of our compensations. Remember, true Hope is when we are able to create a light of service shining with our desires. If I truly understood hope, I would have used my desire to play basketball in the present moment, serving a greater purpose through the assist, the high-five, and the team win.

When we start to train Hope, we start shining in the moment instead of worrying about the future outcome. To fully understand Hope we have to dive deep, and we went a little deeper today!

Consider this analogy. Think of a scuba diver sinking into the depths of the ocean, going deeper and deeper as the water pressure increases. Perhaps today was one of those days. Take time and adjust to the pressure of the deep question: Are your Hopes your Idols?

Embrace the pressure, for when you overcome the uncomfortable nature of the physical or emotional feeling it creates, you will come out the other side with a renewed sense of purpose and Hope!

## ∽ DAY 3 ∾

# Let it Go

Letting it GO!

How are you doing today? These first two days have required you to focus on your perspective of Hope: what the catalyst was, and is now, for your new relationship with Hope.

To review, for us to know Hope and have a clear understanding of it, we must know what Hope is not. Since we have discussed what hope is not, it is time for us to let those perspectives go. If we truly have a desire for Hope to be alive in our life, we need to have a desire for change. Part of this change is accepting what was once our present and is now our past.

Let go of the past memories.

We must have a proper perspective on our memories. Keep memories as memories. While it is harmless to revisit them for insight and encouragement to get you through, it becomes counterproductive when we relive our past and allow those experiences to usurp the present. That kind of mindset could rob you of the possibility of creating something new!

As an example, I was so focused on my cousin Kelly's death that I allowed this same event to come true for myself. I am very fortunate to still be here in the present. When we fixate on the past we allow the past to relive itself over and over again. Reliving can take various forms, including retelling a story, allowing the memory to be at the forefront of our mind, or allowing the past to define your worth. This creates the same type of pain, but every time we revisit it in the present moment we allow ourselves to experience the hurt tenfold.

This is similar to weight lifting. If we continually lift without proper form, we will continue to injure ourselves. Each time, the injury will become worse than it was before. Living in the past creates more hurt than it did when it was its own present moment.

After my alcohol poisoning night, I realized how much life there was to live! I had a choice to allow this life-threatening event to create more pain through the stories I told myself, but I chose differently. I took time off from basketball and reconnected with myself. I grounded my perspective and focused on a better, more fulfilling future. I became a lifeguard that summer and taught swim lessons. Taking on this new adventure connected me to something in my past that was a happy memory, but was also something I could use as Hope for the future. I took swimming lessons in my youth and always dreamt of being a lifeguard. Through reconnecting with my childhood, as a young adult teaching swim lessons, the kids brought me back to the present moment and reminded me of joy.

Allow yourself to travel back to your childhood and the desires you had as a kid. Did you play or imagine yourself becoming a doctor, a teacher, a firefighter?

Discover the reason why you wanted to become those specific professions (or whatever you wanted to become). I imagined that I would become a teacher. While I instruct my clients and share technique and proper skill, I do not consider myself a teacher per se. I am a kettlebell strength coach. I do not need the title of a teacher to teach.

Let go of your past expectations for yourself. You don't need to have that exact title today to determine your purpose and the value you can bring to your life and to many others. We change and evolve as we grow and learn. Let go of the hurt and failures you experienced in the past and rediscover your worth and value in the present moment. Our past memories can act like dark obstacles blocking us from the present moment of Hope.

There is another obstacle that can block us from the light of Hope - idols. Remember, idols are a figment of the mind, a false fantasy.

Let go of the Idols.

Idols create a bright and shiny barrier to Hope, deceiving us from true light. It is very easy to stop and stare with worship. It, too, robs you of creating new possibilities. This is not a simple act to change. But remember your motive. To let go of idols is to have a motive of service, a service of shining for others, versus creating a spotlight for *YOU*.

Letting go of these aspects will take time and practice! It is a moment-to-moment process. It requires mental training to let go of the negative thoughts and replace them with something better, something inspirational and possibly beyond your belief.

I am still practicing the art of letting go by understanding my how my physical abilities can be an inspiration for others to help them achieve and conquer their own physical limits, instead of using it for my own identity and for glory as an athlete. You are much more than the idols in your life and your past memories. You are meant for something much greater than you can ever imagine!

Day 1 and Day 2 both have one thing in common — your deepest desires! Why is it that you hold on to those certain memories? Why do you idolize the things that you hope for?

Explore why you may have certain idols in your life or hold onto certain memories. Play detective within your own life. And have fun as you rediscover you and your desires.

For example, my desire as an athlete was to honor my cousin. I am still able to honor my cousin through my athletics involving water skiing. This sport allows me to live a life full of adventure and passion. My goal now as an athlete is much more than my cousin - it is *you*. My current desire is to inspire you and motivate you through my athletics.

Once you are able to grasp onto your deepest desires it will be easier to let go of the hurtful past, the shiny idols, and fully embrace true Hope. You are worth much more than the worthiness you see in your idols and past memories. Remember, a diamond is only able to shine after being pressurized. I want you to shine! "Letting go" is our pressure system. For us to shine we must experience this pressure. It is uncomfortable at first, but you will be free to shine! You will have the freedom to have a living Hope, a life expecting our desires with confidence.

# ෴ DAY 4 ෴

# Light and Darkness

For Light to exist there has to be darkness.

As you start to practice the art of letting go, it is time to start creating Hope.

For us to shine bright, there will be dark times we will travel through. It doesn't matter if you are a billionaire, a CEO, a mom, or a spouse; no what matter journey you are on there will be dark times. You might be experiencing darkness now. Darkness can take the form of a death in the family, a divorce, the loss of a job, harassment, chronic pain, or suicidal thoughts. These tragic, depressing, and saddening experiences can all lead to the question: "How can there be hope when experiencing this?"

Hope is a choice.

When facing difficult, dark times there are two options: continue to stare into the darkness and become stagnate or start seeking a light source. So how can there be Hope, a light, when it feels impossible? It is a choice. It is a journey to seek and discover the light and define the possible, one step at a time.

The light is something that burns inside of all us. The light encompasses the gifts, the talents, and the traits that make each one of us unique. We need each other in order to shine for one another, thereby leading us to something much better. Seek the Light today and start your journey understanding the helpful Hope.

Today, write down five traits that are your gifts, your qualities, your abilities, and your talents.

1. _____

2. _____

3. _____

4. _____

5. _____

If you are struggling to find five things, ask some of your close friends, family members, and co-workers. They may see something you do not see in yourself (at least, not just yet)! If you still need a little support understanding your fun qualities, search the Internet for the meaning of your name or your Zodiac sign! Find out the meaning of your name! Have fun with this! See how well it may match with your gifts and talents.

As you start this aspect of your journey you may be thinking, "Is it too late for me and my gifts/talents?" The exciting part is when you discover your gifts and talents, the people who you are meant to serve will be ready to receive you and all you have to offer them. You are exactly where you need to be. Continue to trust the journey as you discover more of yourself.

# Shine Bright

Shine Bright!

Are you excited for today? I am! Today is when you start to see that Hope is alive and that it is alive in you! We just need the match to ignite us to shine!

Remember, true Hope is when we are able to create a light of service shining with our desires. It is a light serving each other toward something better, something beyond our own beliefs.

Let's take a look at those five traits you wrote down yesterday. These are gifts. Be thankful for them! But for you to experience these gifts, as they are fully intended, you need to give the gifts freely. For each of these five traits or qualities start thinking about how each one of them can serve others. Now, don't over think this! Keep it as simple as possible.

It could be that you have smile that lights up a room! Or maybe you are a talented writer or a wonderful cook! Here are some Simple Signs of HOPE: a smile, a hug, a thank you letter, saying hello to a stranger, or anything that will brighten someone's day. Sharing your time and showing interest in those you meet is most often remembered long after any physical gift is received.

Now, these are the simple services that give Hope. When you start to understand that you give from a place of service, a place of purpose and satisfaction, you will be able to shine much brighter than you ever anticipated as a result. Once you are able to see your own capabilities you will see what you can offer this world. Give it freely and give it brightly! This is how you are able to create a light using your gifts to serve others.

For us to shine, we need to start looking outside of our circumstances and see how others may be experiencing a different darkness that requires your special gift to help them shine.

Understanding that people need your special gift of light is the match igniting you to shine! Exploring your qualities takes time, and how you create a service will take practice. Allow this time to develop your Light.

How are you going to shine for someone today? It could be one of the simple signs of Hope!

Just simply shine!

# ∞ DAY 6 ∞

# Strength to Shine

Stormy Struggle to Strengthen and Shine Brighter!!!!!

Yesterday we walked through the steps of how to shine for others during their difficult hours of darkness. You may be asking about your own struggle. How do you make it through your own difficult dark times? Once you see you have a purpose to shine for others, you start to see how that is lighting the path for you. This light is showing you step-by-step what to do and how to make your darkest time your brightest moment.

Hope is alive, living through you and guiding you. You will feel something burning inside you that will light the way! For this light to keep burning inside of us, we must live a passionate life. These passions may be the love you have for your spouse or children, the love of creating art, or the love you have for teaching. The examples can go on and on! It is when your gifts and talents are ignited with the powerful action of Love that they truly become something extraordinary.

Love does not simply negate the struggle of darkness. What about the difficulties of going through a miscarriage, a divorce, a death of a loved one, abuse from a family member, a goodbye never said? To live a life full of passion, we must learn how to suffer well. The

25

word passion comes from the Latin root *pati,* meaning suffering or enduring.

How we manage the storms throughout our lives matter.

Yes, there are times in life when it seems unbearable. I know these pains of life all too well. But they can only strengthen you and help you become more of who you are meant to be.

How is this so? There will be times in your life when the darkness is a struggle, a ferocious storm. It may feel like this tempest is trying to blow out your light and kill your passions. What you feel is true! There is a force out there that does not want your gifts to shine. It becomes a battle to fight through the storm of darkness.

I like to think that this turbulent struggle is only strengthening me to shine brighter to live a life full of passion! Think of the reward versus the hardship. It may be strengthening you for something better, something beyond your belief. If you choose to let it change you to become stronger, you are taking the steps toward something beyond your belief.

Using another strength training analogy, let's say you have a certain goal of deadlifting 500 lbs or 30 pull-ups, there will be times when the weight feels unbearable. You have a choice to compensate with the struggle or to struggle and maintain proper form. You will have the strength to continue to shine for your journey, and most importantly, lighting the way for others. This newfound strength may be for something better than what you once hoped for.

Burn Baby Burn! Live a passionate fulfilled life! Now you have the power to light your own path.

# ༚ꙮ Day 7 ꙮ༚

# The Unknown

Embrace the Unknown - Your Future!

Hope for the best, prepare for the worst. Has anyone said this to you? This is not the way we want to condition ourselves for the true meaning of Hope! Hope believes there is a power source lighting the way in the midst of the worst. People say this because it is easy to predict the worst for the future versus the ultimate unknown of any situation. They are focused on the darkness. Hope gives us light for each step. It doesn't light the entire path. All you can do is take one step at a time and embrace the unknown, knowing Hope will light and direct the way toward our dreams.

Remember on the first day, the memory you wrote down and relived to the fullest? The light source wants to give you more of those moments!

"Live a life of wonder, and awe, and expectation of Hope, going confidently in the direction of our dreams." ~ Anna Willard

# Hopes and Dreams

Hopes and Dreams and the difference between the two.

Hope is a glimpse of the possible. Dreams call us to the possibilities.

Hope is a Light. Dreams are a Calling, a calling from a higher power to defy the impossible.

This calling starts to pull on you. It may be a calling to show beauty through your art, to show appreciation of health through athletics, to show love by creating your own family, or to show service through your passions. Take designing and creating clothing as an example of passion. Imagine the amount of love and confidence you would feel when you see someone wearing one of the beautiful items you designed! This calling has a reason and purpose. A purpose we may not see . . . not just yet.

Whatever your calling may be, it is a journey of learning to listen. Learning when it is saying to act, rest, or simply enjoy! However, we live in a society of the American Dream, which is silencing this voice. The American Dream, I believe, has become something of comfort, predictability, and security. Are you following the American Dream of comfort, predictability, and security by taking a safe job, getting married, or going to college?

These goals are not bad. I myself have a college degree.

These goals can turn against us when we use them as a mask to hide our true passions. We forget our dreams and instead fall into this typical American Dream. We live comfortably, acting out predictably, and with a false sense of security. This type of life is stifling. It kills adventure, playfulness, and discovery.

When we truly Dream we chase the infinite possibilities. Dreams are a calling. It calls us to live out our passions while embracing infinite possibilities. If you could do anything in this world what would it be?

Remember how you discovered your light you when we trained your Hopes in Week One? Take your talents, your passions, and gifts - these are your tools to create magic! Now, play and imagine a fulfilling life using your magic with an unlimited amount of possibilities.

## ᭝ DAY 9 ᭜

# Fear

What is holding you back?

You have dreams of the life you feel you deserve. It's exciting, isn't it? Imagine how it would feel to live your wildest dreams? These dreams don't have to be big to be wild. It could simply be a life without chronic pain, having a family, or pursuing the art you want to create. You can pursue any dream, it doesn't need to be big or have a spotlight at the end of it for your dream to be important. If you have a dream, a calling, it is important to live it out.

So what is holding you back?

Fear.

What are you fearful of? Fear of what your parents will think of you? Fear of financial responsibilities? Fear of the journey the Dream is calling you toward?

*Fear of not being enough for your dreams.*

Play with these emotions. They are real. Wrestle with them if you need to! Fight out your Fears and answer your calling.

If we never take the time to face our fears and understand why they exist, the fear itself will paralyze us from progressing toward the life of our dreams. It will allow us to escape the risks, the sacrifices, and the hardships of chasing dreams. Instead of facing our fears, they will become a false companion wrapping us in a security blanket of comfort, never giving us a chance to run after what each of us deserve — a life full of passions, desires, and dreams.

Take the rest of the day to think about your Fears and start giving your dreams a fighting chance. When we face our fears, we start to see that it may not be fear itself. It may be that we fear what is beyond our belief.

Author Marianne Williamson says it perfectly:

"Our deepest fear is not that we are inadequate. Our deepest fear is that we are powerful beyond measure."

## ❧ DAY 10 ❧

# Conquer Fear

Conquer your Fear.

Fears are scary. Why are they so hard to face? Fears reflect our deepest desire.

You may fear what your parents think of you because you desire to have their approval. You may fear money because it might be an idol in your life (remember, idols are also rooted in our deepest desires). You fear the journey because it may be asking you to be more selfless and more of service.

To conquer our fears and let our dreams having a winning chance, there must be a clear understanding of the goal of the dream. What is the mission of the dream? Remember, dreams are a calling and the voice you hear. It is a specific mission for you!

For you to conquer your fears, you need a dream with a powerful mission. Take time today and write down your fears and next to them write down a dream, along with the mission of the dream.

To show how to do this process, below I use money as the first example because it is something simple and easy to understand. The second example goes a little deeper, and with going deeper, it can be a little harder and more emotional.

Fear → Dream → Mission

---

1. Money → Become Millionaire → Give Generously
2. A Parent's Opinion → Nominated Best Personal Trainer → Honor Parents & Work Ethic

Fears will always haunt us if we don't defeat them with a dream. This dream needs to be powerful and have a purpose, a mission to defeat the fears. When you start seeing the strength and power behind your dreams, the fear will flee.

Through the pursuit of our dreams, different fears will continue to try to jump out at us without warning. This is the importance of always dreaming, always listening to the call, and always chasing the infinite possibilities. When we stop dreaming, we surrender to our fears and live them instead of living our wildest dreams.

# ✦ DAY 11 ✦

# Dreams Die

Dreams Die but you are Alive!

Wait, what?! Yes, I know dreams die. I have experienced dying dreams way too many times with my athletics, my career, my health, and my relationships. The very thing you hoped for, your dream, could suddenly turn into divorce papers, your lover cheating on you, the doctor saying you have cancer, or a death in the family.

I was able to have a sense of hope when creating the dream of playing college basketball to honor my cousin Kelly. However, the dream never came true for me. By my senior year of high school, I was still dealing with injuries from the previous season and decided not to participate in any sports that last year.

All disappointments and hardships in life may kill an aspect of our dreams but you are still alive. The difficulty of dying dreams is that it feels like part of us, our spirit, dies with the dream. It is true and the pain is real. Mourn the dream. If you don't take time to grieve, you will never allow yourself — your spirit — to heal, and most importantly, you may never dream again. All you will remember is the pain of the dying dream instead of the joy of dreaming and chasing the infinite possibilities.

When I made the decision to not play basketball, I knew I was saying goodbye to a dream I had for years. It felt like I was dealing with the death of Kelly all over again. I felt like I let him down. These dreams act like a splinter in our foot. Every step we take, we are constantly reminded of our dead dream. With each step, it goes a little deeper.

Instead of our foot, however, dead dreams penetrate our soul. I knew I needed to keep my body healthy and strong for the unknown future. Yet I struggled for many years with the feeling that I failed my cousin Kelly.

The longer it lives inside us, the more it will take control of us. Overt time it will chip away at who we are truly meant to be in this world. We give up simply because one dream didn't come to life and then we stop dreaming. This will steal your gifts, your talents, and your passions. It will dare you to never dream ever again.

Take time today and write down some of your past dreams you once had, or even the death of a dream you may currently be experiencing. This is hard, but like any healing procedure, it is painful at first. Allow the surgeon to go deep into your soul and take the pain, the hurt, and anger, the dream itself. This surgeon will transform it into something much better, something beyond our belief.

Healing gives you the freedom to dream again and to be the person this world needs. By allowing the painful past to heal, you are given a peaceful present, moment-to-moment.

## ✎❧ DAY 12 ❧✎

# Live Present

Mourn the past to live in the present.

Saying goodbye to a long-held dream is extremely challenging. Let it go. Let it go moment-to-moment, day-by-day, memory-by-memory. I had to do this with my dream of being a collegiate athlete. I had to let it go.

Just because I was able to let go of my dream my senior year does not mean I still don't have to do it in the present moment as well. I have to do this every time I am asked if I played a college sport. I simply let it go with a big smile on my face and say, "No, I never was a collegiate athlete."

Release it and start living again in the present moment. This current moment has something for you - the gift to start dreaming again! It will revel to you a little nugget of truth for future moments. Don't miss it!

Listen for the calling. It has something for you — specifically for you — at this present moment. We simply have to let go and be open to the infinite possibilities. You may even start to see that the root of your dream is still alive while living in the present. The mission of the dream is still there.

When dreams die, the dream is simply redirecting us to the live the mission of it, not the dream itself. The path of your dream is taking a different direction than you may have anticipated, but it is the only way to keep the real mission of it alive.

During my senior year, I was open to the possibility of something beyond my belief and enrolled in the Spokane Lilac Beauty Pageant. Overnight I went from athletics shorts and sneakers to high-heeled shoes and fancy gowns. The banquet's theme that year was to give a speech on "what makes Spokane such a magical place to live." By this time in my life, I could not wait to leave Spokane and didn't appreciate growing up there until I gave this speech. (Make sure you watch the entire speech. It is important! I was living out a dream I didn't even know I had).

At the time, I didn't realize it, but I was able to honor my cousin Kelly! I told a story of reliving a magical memory of racing on the ice rink with my cousin Kelly when my friends gave me a surprise birthday party. It brought Kelly's spirit back to life; his gift of living a playful and adventurous life. I had fulfilled my mission. I was able to honor my cousin Kelly, and the life he lived, my senior year of high school in a much bigger way than becoming a collegiate athlete.

Be open to the mission by living it daily. I don't have to be a millionaire to live a life of generosity. I don't need to earn the best personal trainer award to give honor to my parents.

With this mindset, you can focuses on the process, not the result. It's about creating the light instead earning the spotlight! You have the end goal in mind: the mission. The beauty of being open daily is following the call step-by-step. Allow the pull on your heart to direct your steps.

When we start allowing and accepting a different journey for our dreams, we start to see the magic happen. People will enter your life to help your mission! Most importantly, you will discover a new strength deep inside yourself. A different journey allows different people to cross your path and enter your world. You get to dream with them! And together you are able to accomplish a much bigger mission. Together, you accomplish your wildest dreams. It may not be who you thought, but it may be exactly who you need in your life.

You find a new strength living inside yourself, a strength you wouldn't have known if your journey hadn't changed. I didn't know I could give a speech. This newfound strength will give you the tools and skills to live out your wildest dreams. It could be something far better, something beyond belief! Today take time today to dive back into your past dreams and look for the blessings in disguise. Start to see who entered into your life as a result.

Who helps you to keep dreaming? Did you discover a new strength? It could be the newfound love you have for your child after a miscarriage, the love you have for a new marriage after a divorce, the newfound creativity for your art, or the physical strength gained after an injury.

You may not have even realized, but as hard as it was or currently is, you are stronger from the redirection of your dreams. This new strength is exactly what you need to manage a life full of wonder.

# ᥫᵉ Day 13 ᥫᵉ

# Power to Dream

Power to Dream again.

How do you start to dream again? It is scary to dream again. You feel vulnerable and may be asking yourself what if they don't come true like last time? Or you may fear the pain of dreaming again, period. You don't even know if you have the strength or the courage for another dream and the possibility that it might die. Especially after dealing with a tough reality, you may only have enough strength to get through a "normal" day. But simply existing is not living. This can be extremely hard. Yes. I know.

For us to dream again, we have to completely let go of controlling our dreams and be content with it. We need to develop a peaceful past, trusting something better. That something beyond our belief is at work. Again, this takes time. It is a healing process. Dreaming again will expedite the process.

The secret to dreaming again is to develop a childlike spirit. Many people cannot do this without being around children. The innocent mind is powerful, and children are the only ones who have a true and pure innocent mind. To dream again we need children encouraging us to chase the infinite possibilities. It does not matter your age, whether it be 60 or 16-years-old, but the truth is, children bring out a side of us we forgot all about: our innocence.

Even if you've accomplished all your dreams (awesome!), we need dreams to keep us progressing through life. Just like movement and exercise keeps our bodies alive, dreams keep our spirits alive — our gifts, our talents, our passions!

So go have some fun today! Go be a child again. This may be through the art of coloring. It could be telling an imaginary story. Or it could be as simple as taking a child on a walk and seeing the world through his/her eyes. They see the beauty that we have forgotten.

Beauty also inspires us to dream again. Here in Seattle we have the most breathtaking landscape, from the magnificent mountains to the peaceful lakes to the iconic cityscape. If you live here you must take full advantage of this. For example, today I wrote a portion of this book sitting in my car with all the doors open at one of my favorite parks.

Beauty is a lovely welcome to the immeasurable possibilities of life. We forget the worries of the world by taking in the captivating beauty. It lets our minds wonder about the powerful artist behind the inspiring landscape. When was the last time you simply sat and quietly watched a sunset or sunrise? No interruptions, no distractions, no words, just answered the beautiful call to simply enjoy the moment. Once we are open, we start to see nature with infinite possibilities again. You see the tree's invitation to climb its trunk for a different view. The oceans that want to support you, asking you to let go of your baggage. The sky asking you to use your imagination and tell her untold story as her clouds dance in the sky.

We cannot help but play when we accept this invitation. We become physically active again, running, skipping, laughing, climbing, and swimming through nature. When we are physically active, we start to see that the youth of our spirit is still alive. We start to feel the infinite possibilities again.

See the world through the innocence of a child.
Open the beautiful invitation from nature.
And create a playful spirit again.

# A False Fantasy

A False Fantasy.

Daydreaming. There is something magical about wondering what is to come. I love being outside under the big blue sky and watching the clouds roll by, or being out in the middle of a wheat field and feeling the possibilities. Dreams are wonderful and glorious, but they will remain dreams if there is no action behind them to support them. The voice is calling you to act.

If there is no action to our dreams, they don't just remain innocent dreams. They can quickly become a false fantasy. This can be a very slippery slope. It is far too easy to have a wild dream and fantasize about our dreams and calling. When there is no action to support our dream, we slowly start training this false fantasy instead of the dream itself.

When training this false fantasy, we create a delusion and hope for an artificial result. Remember, the fundamental principle of Hope is guiding us step-by-step, moment-by-moment.

We start manipulating the calling because it does not align with this false fantasy. Worse, we try to control the dreams of others to make sure it aligns with the artificial result we so desperately think we want. We don't even realize what we are doing! We are still hoping and dreaming, right? We are hoping and dreaming for the end result. One of the fundamental principles of Hope is that it is lighting the way one step at a time. But we take it and try to shine the false fantasy all the way, lighting a path to what we think our dreams should be, to prove that we were right in our dream destiny!

Bottom line, we control our dreams. They are a calling and pull from a force greater than us. To live a life beyond our wildest dreams there has to be something bigger than us. I have done this with a past relationship. I took this light of Hope and tried to shine it to the end result of marriage. As a result, I created a false fantasy of the gentleman. I allowed this false fantasy of this man to become more real in my mind than the man present in my life.

I missed out on the opportunity of truly getting to know him. Instead I ended up causing more hurt and pain as I tried to manipulate him into this false fantasy. We both had our dream destinies but our dreams were different. When each of our dream destinies did not become alive in our life, we both would try to control one another, causing more pain and hurt. As a result, we lost sight of the Hope. We were busy trying to fix "us." We didn't hear our calling and the dream was lost.

To fully believe in our dreams, we have to actually *live* our dreams. We believe through our actions. Remember, the dream's mission is important to live. The magic is in the doing. The magic is in the act of believing.

Believe. Hope will guide the way.
Dreams will direct our steps.
Believe your actions will be enough.

# Behavior Reflects Belief

Behavior reflects Beliefs.

Sometimes our beliefs are not fully realized, they're a bit uncertain. We may have an idea of what we believe in or what we want to believe. To truly understand our conviction, it is important that we see our actions as a mirror reflecting what we believe in the present moment. It is not what we want to believe in the future.

Imagine a beautiful, still body of water. It has a perfect reflection of the sky with every detail, down to the tiniest cloud. The calm captivates you, and you forget if you are looking up at the sky or down at the body of water. The reflection is perfect. Similar to this perfect, calm reflection, our behaviors reflect our beliefs. We need to sit still in order to see the reflection of our beliefs demonstrated in our behavior.

We constantly fill our days with activity, avoiding our reflection. This is constantly adding wave after wave, never giving us a chance to see our beliefs. We do this because we may fear seeing the ugliness it could reveal. It could be things that are hard to face.

Just like facing our fears, we must face our flaws.

If we have the capacity to live a life beyond our wildest dreams we need to have the courage to look at some of the ugly parts of our life first. Through this process of learning and admitting areas of improvement, we are able to progress to something better and beyond our own belief.

First we need stillness. We need to calm ourselves from the busyness of life. Once we are able to become calm and quiet, we start to see our beliefs living throughout our routine days. Most importantly, we need the courage to look at our reflection, our complete self, the good and the bad.

Schedule time to sit and reflect, like you would schedule a meeting to discuss business. Take the same focus and energy to schedule time for focusing on the busyness from the actions of your life. This could be through journaling and simply writing down all your actions you did throughout the day. Or imagine you are in a movie - your life is the story line with you as the main character. Replay your day(s) and see what it reveals to you.

The longer you sit in stillness away from all of your other obligations, the more you are able to spend time reflecting on the smallest details of your day. Examples of daily details include making the bed in the morning, or brushing your teeth at night. Review the details of how you spent your money. What types of food you ate and which you enjoyed most? Reflect on how you interacted with your co-workers and your loved ones. How you treated the clerk at the grocery store or your waiter at dinner last night. What do these actions reveal about you? This is not an easy process. I regularly do this; and most of the time I am disappointed with what I discover about my belief in myself. It is through this process that I become aware of how my actions do not align with my beliefs.

During this task, I have two options. One, ignore what I see and keep pretending it will work itself out. Or two, take action knowing who I want to be and believe in something different about myself. Once you see your actions you will see these are your beliefs. If you believe you will be debt free, you will spend your money according to your budget to become debt free. If you believe you will be healthy, you will eat healthy. If you believe you deserve a promotion at work, your work ethic will prove you deserve that promotion.

This process opens up our eyes to the root of our beliefs. It can be a little shocking because some things you thought you believed are not necessarily true. Instead, it is merely a desire to believe. For example, you believe forgiveness is vital, but you still have yet to forgive others who wronged you and forgive yourself for your own flaws. Your actions articulate that forgiveness is actually the reverse of your perceived belief. Another example, you believe health is essential, but you actions demonstrate the opposite. You have yet to exercise or eat vegetables on a regular basis. The list could go on and on.

Writing these actions down is a powerful tool. It allows you to see everything about yourself. Most importantly, it shows who you believe yourself to be. Again, this can be shocking at first. Take time to allow yourself the freedom to become the person you always believed yourself to be. Have the courage to look at your flaws head-on.

Today, write down some of your flaws. This is very uncomfortable. It is like hanging out the dirty laundry. Don't worry, once you are able to face your imperfections, you will shine brighter than you ever anticipated. Now that you have shared your flaw(s), next write what your actions say about your beliefs. Write about how you want to change this belief through your future actions. After jotting down your new game plan, write down your new belief.

This starts transforming your flaws into something admirable. Here is a simple example: Flaw: Ignoring your barista while being on the phone.

Belief: The items on my phone are more important than the human being who is right in front of me wanting to serve me at that current moment.

Change of Action: Looking the barista in the eyes when ordering. Acknowledging him or her with a smile and a thank you.

New Belief: I value the smallest act of service the barista is able to give me through fulfilling my coffee order. I value him/her as a person, and I'm thankful for this small act of service.

Believe by taking action in your life. Trust that you are designed for something much more beyond your belief.

# ✤ DAY 16 ✤

# The Sacrifice

Believe in the Sacrifice.

Day one of believing was a big day! So if you need extra time to dwell on it, give yourself the freedom to do this! As you continue this journey of understanding your beliefs, you will start to see the difference between what you believe and what you want to believe. Something is holding you back from changing your desires into something you believe in.

It is the sacrifice. The work to overcome the challenge. The work of changing our flaws into something admirable. You may want to be healthy, but you are not willing to sacrifice the nights out with your friends and the poor eating and drinking habits that accompany it. You enjoy and believe those present moments are more important than having a healthier lifestyle.

Can you imagine if you sacrificed just one night out for a good night's slumber and, consequently, having the energy to hike up a mountain to see the sunrise the next day? Imagine the fresh air kissing your skin, welcoming you to a new way of living. Imagine the sunrise giving you a wink, saying, "I have so much more for you! This is just the beginning." Imagine the mountain supporting you, giving you a view you never thought you would see in person.

The gift of life has some incredible things to give you and health is one of them.

There are many other aspects of changing our wants into believing. It could be making the sacrifice of not eating out, or not shopping, to pay off debt. To be able to save enough money to take your entire extended family on a vacation. The sacrifice is hard but the reward is so much more than we could ever imagine! So, as you start to see where you may need to make sacrifices in your life, keep dreaming and hoping this will change your life for the better!

The fun part about the sacrifice you are committed to make is laying down the foundation for you to have a platform. This platform allows you to give to those you love, or even a complete stranger, a taste of Hope. As you believe by changing your actions, you start to live and demonstrate Hope to others.

Think back to yesterday's example: the barista! Can you imagine if you had the freedom to give this complete stranger a $200 tip? Especially after talking to her about her dreams and the career she wants to pursue while managing a part-time job and attending school full-time. This barista would never forget you! Your act of love. Your act of giving. Your act of support. Your act of believing!

Because you first believed in the sacrifice, it gave you the freedom to perform an admirable act. You were able to act by believing in others. But first you had to believe in yourself and believe in the sacrifice. Believing, the sacrifice soon becomes an offering, an offering of Hope.

Now imagine how you will feel after sharing the success of your sacrifice with others! It could be how you will feel when you reach your physical health goal. Pay for someone else to join boot camp or personal training to receive the same joy and freedom you were able to experience.

When we believe in the sacrifice, we believe in more than ourselves. We are empowered to start believing in others, and that they too will have the same experience of believing and having a sense of Hope.

## ❧ DAY 17 ஐ

# Your Journey

Believe in your own journey.

Going back to yesterday, we all have sacrifices to make but each of us will have different ones to make. The sacrifice your dream is calling you to make is a journey designed specifically for you! This journey of sacrifice you are about to embark on is your journey where you will develop your weakness into strengths and your strengths into an incredible power.

The dreams that are calling you, pulling on your heart, know you by name and call _____ (fill in the blank with your name) to a journey only _____ (your name again) can travel.

This journey is your journey. As we start to believe in ourselves and take each step the light of Hope is guiding us, and we can sometimes see the journeys of others. This can be people joining us on our journey, or others whose dreams are creating a similar journey to ours. A journey that you may not have thought you would be traveling. A journey of marriage, family, children, the new home, the podium, the promotion - again the list could go on.

Simply because someone else is living your dreams and aspirations does not mean you won't. It is simply not your time. Continue the journey and trust that it will equip you with everything you will need for your wildest dreams to come to life. When dwelling on other people's dreams and their calling, jealousy, envy, and bitterness start to fill the mind. These will slowly quiet the dream's calling, and you will lose sight of Hope lighting the way. Then there is no movement, no progression to fulfill your wildest dreams. Sometimes that is better, something that is beyond your own belief.

Comparison starts to set in. The fixation on what others have that you perceive as better will stunt the growth of your thoughts and take your focus away from your gifts and your strengths. Instead of believing in ourselves, we simply sit back and watch the journey/dreams of others unfold before us. Instead of allowing the journey to transform us and turn our weakness into our greatest strength and our strengths into an incredible power, we become a victim of "woe is me."

We become a victim and our own villain in our story instead of allowing and trusting the journey to change us into a hero. This "woe is me" concept cuts us off from all the possibilities, all the infinite possibilities. It allows us to sit comfortably with our flaws and we forget there is Hope!

We forget the power of believing. Believing in the journey. Slowly we will change our actions into actions of disbelief. It could be the simple act of not making your bed in the morning, not doing the dishes, or not brushing your teeth.

Three years ago, I began to turn away from believing in my journey. Slowly, I began giving up on my dreams and not taking the extra time to make my bed, and not brushing my teeth. (I use these as examples simply because I have lived them). Unfortunately, because I was allowing my dreams to die a slow death, I soon became injured. I was not taking care of the smallest details of the day and as a result I did not take care of my own health.

I have to admit, it was all because my dreams were being redirected. My journey was taking a turn that I did not want to make. I declined a future with man whom I thought I would marry. I thought we would live happily ever after, water-skiing our summers away. But this was not the outcome. I said no to who I thought was suppose to be my future husband, with the glimpse of someone better.

By saying no, I started to believe there was someone better, someone beyond my belief; I thought they would show up that year, that week, that day. Believing is a step-by-step process. Simply because it did not show up and still hasn't yet does not mean it won't.

But at times I compared myself to all my friends who were getting married. Instead of enjoy their wedding celebrations, I was disappointed that I was single. Although still single today, I continue to believe I will be with someone who is beyond my wildest dreams. Embracing myself fully in the present moment, I know my journey of singleness is preparing me for something and someone far beyond what I could ever imagine.

Trust that your dreams are directing you to your deepest desires. Simply because it arrives in another's journey first does not mean it won't for you! The journey has something to teach you, something to equip you with, and will give you exactly what you need to live a life full of wonder, excitement, and pure joy. Allow the journey to strengthen you to become the hero in your life and the lives of others. By trusting the powerful unknown, you allow a cleansing flow to be transformed to become exactly who you are meant to be. You offer your weakness to become transformed into one of your greatest strengths. *YOU* start to become someone beyond your wildest dream.

Your dreams are calling you by name! They are calling you to become someone better, someone far beyond you ever thought of by yourself. Here is a little fun activity for you to feel how your dreams are calling you at this present moment.

Fill in the blank with your dream, your name, and an action toward your dream.

_____ (your dream) is calling _____ (your name) to be _____ (an action toward your dreams) for something beyond your imagination.

Examples ~

My dream of <u>being married</u> is calling <u>Anna Willard</u> to be <u>patient and be content with her singleness</u> for something beyond her imagination.

My dream of <u>living healthy</u> is calling <u>Anna Willard</u> to be <u>diligent and disciplined daily with her exercise routines</u> for something beyond her imagination.

This journey is your journey. Embrace it to the fullest and enjoy every present moment.

# Feelings

Believe even when you don't feel like it.

There are still many times I wake up in the morning and think I could sleep a couple of seconds more if I left without making my bed. Or at night I allow my mind to play this rehearsal, "I am too tired to brush my teeth, I worked hard today and need the extra few minutes of sleep."

All because I was not with the man I thought was my life-mate. I was not allowing the dreams to redirect my journey. I wanted to give up. Three years ago, I allowed myself to travel down this path of non-believing. I constantly have to change my thoughts and my actions back to believing in myself through these small acts of self-care (like brushing my teeth). They help me maintain my discipline to sustain my health and it keeps my dreams alive.

When we believe the sacrifice is worth every minute of our work and discipline, we start to see how the sacrifice is an offering. There will be times when we may feel like it is not worth it. But it is! Our feelings will not want to make the sacrifice because the sacrifice is an offering of our weakness.

Similar to the little rationalization I made to myself almost every night three years ago, our feelings will try to play a song and dance throughout our thoughts and tell us differently. They will try to have you go back to long nights of consuming unhealthy foods and beverages, simply because there is instant gratification through this process. It keeps our weakness hidden and protected, and your feelings are happy again!

Everyone has their own journey. I am simply using this as an example of how our feelings want the instant gratification and our weakness wants to stay hidden. When we fall into this trap, we forget about the reward from the sacrifice. The only way to mute our feelings is through action. When we physically move and do the smallest task leading us to our dreams, our feelings simply shut up and are reminded of the unknown reward that will be at the end of the journey.

When we take action we continue to see Hope lighting the next step. Or it may start shining brighter, allowing us to see a little further than anticipated. Either way, when we start acting in our full belief, Hope starts shining bright for us, and through us it will shine.

At the same time, the dream will continue to call you. This voice will become more and more clear when we are able to quiet ourselves and understand our beliefs. Again, through the act of believing the dream, our dreams may start to call us to something bigger, something beyond our wildest belief.

The bigger the dream the bigger the sacrifice the dream is asking us to make. It is calling us to be strong for the journey ahead. Again, sacrifices are hard. So hard that many people are not willing to make them.

They would rather satisfy their feelings with instant gratification, and with nothing waiting for them in the near future, beyond the predictable pleasure. They keep their weakness hidden and never allow their self to truly develop the strength to be strong for a life that is beyond their wildest dreams. When we start to make even the smallest sacrifices, our dreams continue to guide us and ask if we can handle even more growth.

What goes on in the gym when a client becomes stronger? I add more weight to their barbell or have them "bell up" (go up to the next Kettlebell weight).

There will be many times when you will want the easy way out, but I will remind you - you will be settling for less. You will only experience something that is merely good. You will miss all the wonders of experiencing something beyond your wildest dreams.

## ⁓⊛ DAY 19 ⊛⁓

# Beyond Good
# Beyond Great

Believe beyond good and believe beyond great!

All right! Let's travel back in time again! Remember a time when you were able to accomplish something amazing! It could have been when you were able to achieve a college athletic scholarship, you were rewarded for your art, or maybe it is not you, but your children, who were able to achieve something great! These things are all awesome! But if we dwell on great events we take away potential possibilities from the current moment. This can end up tricking us!

There are times for celebration, like graduating from high school. However, if the following year all you do is remember the greatness you were able to accomplish in high school, you won't see the opportunities that are sitting right in front of you. Again, going back to the analogy of weight lifting, if I allowed one of my clients to remain lifting the same weight for weeks, months, and years, they would never progress to their physical goals. They would never live to their full potential.

Great events in life are meant for celebration! So, embrace that present moment and celebrate! Embrace all the work it took to get there! Understand the journey doesn't end there. It is just a new beginning to a different part of your life, a different terrain on your journey. This new beginning will uncover new strengths, new joys, and new wonders of the world.

But we get stuck in past celebrations, past successes and past achievements. Slowly, it becomes a self-righteous act. Being on a pedestal of success is great! Enjoy the moment, but then get off and start working toward the next dream, the next goal of serving others along the way. When we stay on this high of accomplishments, it does not allow us to discover our true power. Instead of continuing to believe in ourselves through continuous action, we start believing the past accomplishments were all we were meant for in life.

But you are still alive and the dream is not just calling you, it has a different message for you - a different daily message to live its full mission.

During water ski tournaments, in addition to competing, I am either helping the scorekeeper or I am one of the judges. Each of us works toward the goal of running a successful tournament. It is out of serving each other we are able to keep the tournaments running and keep the sport alive. Yes, we all want to compete and improve in the sport, but we all want each other to do the same! This is the fuel that drives all of us to stay long weekends working the tournaments and competing at the same time. If we were to take this same approach, living every day with the mission in mind, who knows of all the accomplishment, all the greatness, you could live day in and day out.

## ❧ DAY 20 ❧

# Wow the World

Believe in the transformation and wow the world.

With each type of terrain the journey of believing will lead us to, we develop different skills, strengths, and appreciation for life. Sometimes we don't want to finish or end a certain part of the journey because we know this new terrain will demand a new skill and strength. This could be anything, like entering college, a marriage, or your promotion.

To survive this new terrain we have to surrender our weakness and allow the journey to transform it into an incredible power. The new terrain will challenge us to grow; it is the challenges we need to grow. It is the challenges we need to grow into the person we always dreamed of becoming. When we believe in the transformation, we believe in becoming more of who we are meant to be.

Sometimes the journey of believing challenges us in ways we never thought possible. It could be how you may have anticipated to be married or to receive the promotion or the trophy by this time in your life. It could be that you are able to retire at a young age but are surprised by your boredom. It may be that the dreams have called you to believe in a different journey, a journey that may not have the husband or the promotion.

When you start to realize you don't necessarily need these things to have an epic life, then you start to see yourself as your own hero! You see your own strengths and the incredible power the journey of believing has allowed you to develop.

Maybe you feel you have traveled all the journeys there are in life, and you have accomplished all your dreams. Or maybe you feel it is too late. It is never too late, because there is still a light living inside of you. Hope is still lighting a way and the dreams continue to pull on your heart.

But you don't see a path before you. The journey has given you all the tools and strength to create a path for you, and most importantly, for others, to travel. When you see it is not only for you to travel, but to help others, it will empower you and motivate you to a different level.

When you know people need your gifts and talents to create this new path - people who you have never met and may never meet. It will help you take the next scary, challenging step in your journey. These lives will be forever changed because you saw the hopeful light, and your heard the dream calling you to act. Most importantly, you have the courage to believe and demonstrate your belief in yourself through your daily actions.

The journey has transformed you from follower to leader.

It is time to create this adventurous new life, something that is better and is beyond your belief. You have the power to do this, to live your wildest dreams. The journey is asking you to embrace this new power and take the next step towards your beautiful life.

# You Are Enough

Believe your actions are enough!

You are enough. You are enough for something beyond your wildest dreams. Right now, at this present moment, you are enough. You have all the tools and gifts to live this current moment to the fullest. The present moment has a golden nugget of truth to give you. We are only able to receive this gift when we believe we are enough and become open to the infinite possibilities.

When we allow ourselves to let go of the past and forget the worries of the future, we are able to live openly and in the present. We become open to all the possibilities from the present moment. We not only receive, but also give. We give our gifts and talents, confidently knowing it is enough for the present moment.

The gifts and talents you give are exactly what the present moment needs. Believing is acting. Taking action believing we are enough.

I believe this present moment is allowing me, _____ (your name), to see that I am enough, that I have been given the strength for the journey and the dreams that are calling me.

I believe this present moment is strengthening me, _____ (your name), to love others deeper and give them a sense of Hope.

I believe in you _____ (your name)

I believe in you _____ (your name)

I believe in you _____ (your name)

Trust your past has given you all the tools you need for this current moment in time. Trust this moment in time is continuing to prepare you for your future. Be present knowing there is power in the unknown at this current moment in time.

By believing you are enough, you start to live with open hands ready to give and ready to receive a life that is far beyond your wildest dreams.

Hope will always guide the way.
Your dreams are directing your steps.
Believe you are enough.

You are exactly what the world needs.
Now go live with open hands,
open to receive the light of others and
be open to give your light brightly

Trust in the powerful unknown.

# The end, but also the beginning of something beautiful

Thank you for doing this 21-day fitspirational journey. These past 21 days are just the beginning of amazing things happening in your life.

As we complete this 21-day fitspirational, it is time for me to introduce you to my dear friend Portia. The beautiful spirit of Portia: the end to a beautiful life, but the beginning of something better, something beyond my belief.

Portia was a childhood, neighborhood friend who we rarely saw, as her time was shared between her divorced parents. But every moment we had together was a magical moment filled with Portia's excitement to see the "Willards!" As we started to grow into our young adult years, our times together were very limited. This made each visit even more magical. Portia always made each one of us feel like we were on top of the world when we were around her.

She supported my brothers and sisters each individually, and at the same time encouraged us to maintain our friendships as a family. She supported me with my basketball adventures during high school. No matter what or where each of us was in life, I knew Portia was cheering me on to continue my journey.

After graduation and not obtaining my goal of playing college basketball, I had no real desire to attend school. It was during one of those magical moments with Portia when she told me how she wished she had gone to college right after high school. Being confident and comfortable with her own journey of no college degree, she empowered me to take action to further my education.

So, off to Eastern Washington University I went for a degree in Exercise Science with the hopes of becoming a Physical Therapist. During college I had many adventures with water-skiing, taking me places I would never have dreamed of like Naples, Maine. I enjoyed every summer I had through college, but when it was time to return to my books I found myself discouraged and was ready to quit. I remember a time when Portia and her mom picked me up from the airport. I was so excited to tell her and her mother all the wonders I was able to experience that summer. Both of them were thrilled with joy for me and the journey life was giving me.

This was the last summer adventure in Maine and I was about to enter one more year of college with no desire to finish. Reluctant to return to school, Portia gave me yet another magical moment during that car ride home. Portia reminded me of the importance of the knowledge and the opportunities a college degree provides.

I graduated that spring and started to chase my dreams both professionally and with my athletics. I started to fulfill a dream living in the Emerald City, also known as Seattle, Washington. I was working as a personal trainer, and during my free time I was water- skiing! I was living on cloud nine! Thrilled I was living my dreams!

But unfortunately, right before the water ski season started, I searched for a flight back to Spokane.

Portia had dealt with chronic back pain five plus years. To cope with her pain, she took prescription pain meds. Unfortunately, one prescription was written incorrectly and sweet Portia's life ended May 2011. I was searching for a flight to attend her funeral.

Shocked and devastated, I struggled with the reality that the person who gave the extra fuel to continue my journey was gone! I dedicated that water-ski season to Portia. I was blessed to have been able to compete, and to qualify for both regionals and nationals. It was out of gratitude for the little gifts she always gave me.

Shortly after the water ski season ended, I started to deal with chronic back pain myself. The pain was so great, it forced me to take time off work. The only way I was able to return to work was with the assistance of pain meds. I didn't think much of this at first, but after three months of living on pain meds. It started to seem all too familiar to me. I was reliving part of Portia's life unconsciously.

Remembering the lesson I learned with Kelly's death, I changed my focus to the life Portia lived. I decided to live out the gifts Portia gave me. I remembered how Portia gave the extra fuel for my passions. Determined to have a different story, I went off the pain medications and used food as my medicine.

Determined to exercise and train again, I discovered the Turkish Get Up. This movement gave me hope. I soon was able to move without pain! After long hours of practicing the Turkish Get Up, I felt strong enough to learn the kettlebell swing. This newfound power gave me another fuel source physically, mentally, emotionally, and spiritually to continue the journey chasing my dreams.

Still, to this day, this movement gives me Hope. At the darkest moment of my life, I knew if I simply did a Turkish Get Up instead of giving up I would have the strength physically, mentally, and spiritually to face the daily challenges of life.

I am now 30 years old, the same age that our sweet beautiful Portia left her physical body. I dedicate this 21-day fitspirational not only to her but also to *YOU* and encourage you to continue your journey just as Portia's spirit continues to do this for me.

As we end this 21-day fitspirational, I prayerfully meditate that you are able to live a life full of adventures, passion, and wonder from the amazing power in the *unknown*.

# Next Steps to Spark Your Journey ~

As you start training your hopes and dreams, I encourage you to train your body with the Turkish Get Up movement. If you don't know what this is, check out this amazing Kettlebell exercise.[1] This link will lead you to a YouTube playlist. It will teach you step-by-step the Turkish Get Up. Again, my goal with teaching this type of exercise is to give you a sense of hope and a taste of your powerful self.

Thank you again for reading this fispirational. I would love to hear from you and how this book helped train your hopes and dreams to believe! You can email me at Coachwillard10@gmail.com! Title the email with "ironwilltrain" in reference to this book. I am excited to hear from you!

Sign up for Willard's Wisdom Wednesday to read weekly insights with kettlebell training, nutrition, and healthy habits.[2]

---

1 https://www.youtube.com/playlist?list=PLJ8VCVMJLJVIILy2lIkN6cFbyQ8Mj5a8v
2 http://forms.aweber.com/form/27/317004527.htm

# IronWillTrain

HOPE

DREAM

unknown

BELIEVE

# About the Author
## ~ Anna Willard

A Washingtonian born and raised in Spokane, she is the oldest from a family of five. She currently lives in Seattle as a Kettlebell Strength Coach.

Her inspiration is drawn from personal training and coaching over these last six years. Seeing first hand how hopes and dreams go hand in hand with physical fitness, she decided to write this book.

She currently trains in Belltown. For more information about training, go to her website www.annawillard.com

Writing this book inspired her to apply to graduate school. She will earn her Masters in Psychology and Theology at The Seattle School of Theology and Psychology starting fall of 2017!

Ephesians 1:18 I pray that the eyes of your heart may be enlightened in order that you may know the hope to which he has called you, the riches of his glorious inheritance in his holy people,

67188685R10046

Made in the USA
San Bernardino, CA
20 January 2018